ACTION FRENCH!

What is *Action French!*?

Action French! is designed as a 'treasure chest' of activities and games for learning French. Use it as an extra resource in a class or group, or at home with your own children. You don't have to be fluent in French – learn along with the children! You can adapt the material for a range of ages, from 3 to 10. Pick and choose from the ideas here to create your own language sessions. Even if you only use one idea and it's successful, that's fine!

Before you start – familiarise yourself with the contents of the *Action French* pack.

In the book itself you will find:
★ Words and Phrases (page 2 and 3)
★ Activities and Games (pages 4 to 10)
★ Rhymes and Songs (pages 11 and 12)

In the centre of the book you will find a 'pull-out' section which includes:
★ Treasure Hunt board game
★ Body and Clothes (back of board game)
★ Labels for the house
★ Themed flash cards

On the inside covers of the book are:
★ Supercat mask and finger puppet templates
★ Badges and game counters (back cover flap)
★ Instructions on how to use the templates, back cover flap and pull-out pages.

In addition there is:
★ **A recording** – with all the words and phrases, and the rhymes and songs, including 'karaoke' versions to sing along to.
★ **A poster** – of weather, days of the week, months of the year, the seasons, numbers, and the alphabet.

Children learning languages

The earlier you start learning a language, the better. Children are curious about new people and places and are not at all inhibited about making strange sounds. They don't worry about making mistakes and they are proud of their achievements. These are all wonderful language-learning qualities! The trick is to make sure children enjoy the experience of learning. That is the aim of *Action French!*

★ Keep the French sessions short but as regular as possible.
★ Stimulate all the children's senses, with sounds, colours, shapes, smells and movement. The book has ideas on this.
★ If you only have one child, invite a friend over to the French sessions. It's more fun to learn in a small group.
★ Take every opportunity to have a genuine 'French experience', meeting French people or travelling to France or another French-speaking country.

This is **Superchat** (Supercat). Look out for him and his worst enemy **Monstrerat** (Monsterat), and family. They only speak French!

SALUT!

1

Words and Phrases

Here are some basic words and expressions which can be taught using the *Activities and Games* (page 4). Listen to them on the recording to practise their pronunciation. You can refer to them at any time so you don't need to learn them all at once! *You will find other important words on the labels, the flash cards, the poster, and the back of the board game. They are also on the recording.*

Saying hello

bonjour	hello
salut	hi
au revoir	goodbye
bonsoir	good evening
bonne nuit	good night
comment t'appelles-tu?	what's your name?
je m'appelle	my name is
quel âge as-tu?	how old are you?
j'ai… ans	I'm…
voici…	this is…
ça va?	how are you?
très bien, merci	very well, thanks
ça ne va pas!	awful!

Family and friends

maman	mum
papa	dad
ma mère	my mother
mon père	my father
ma sœur	my sister
mon frère	my brother
ma grand-mère	my grandmother
mon grand-père	my grandfather
mon amie *(girl)*	my friend
mon ami *(boy)*	my friend
mes amies *(girls)*	my friends
mes amis *(boys, or mixed)*	my friends

General expressions

oui	yes
non	no
merci	thank you
s'il te plaît	please
s'il vous plaît *(polite)*	please
ici/là	here/there
c'est	it's
ce sont	these are
il y a	there is
je vais	I'm going
je suis	I am
j'ai	I have
je n'ai pas	I haven't

Shopping and eating

je voudrais…	I'd like…
ça	that
petit/petite	little
grand/grande	big
voilà	here you are
j'ai faim	I'm hungry
j'ai soif	I'm thirsty
j'aime	I like
je n'aime pas	I don't like
c'est combien?	how much is it?
c'est tout?	is that all?

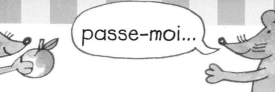

Useful instructions

passe-moi	pass me
apporte-moi	bring me
prends	take (it)
vite!	quickly!
prêt/prête?	ready?
à moi	my turn
à toi	your turn
j'ai gagné!	I've won!
bravo!	well done!
très bien	very good
super	great
allons-y!	let's go!
j'arrive	I'm coming
dors bien	sleep well
bon appétit	enjoy your meal

Pastimes

je lis	I read (or I'm reading)
je regarde la télé	I watch TV
j'écoute la musique	I listen to music
je chante	I sing
je danse	I dance
je joue	I play
je joue au football	I play football
je ne fais rien!	I don't do anything!
j'aime lire	I like reading
j'aime regarder la télé	I like watching TV
j'aime écouter la musique	I like listening to music
j'aime chanter	I like singing
j'aime danser	I like dancing
j'aime jouer	I like playing
j'aime jouer au football	I like playing football

Useful questions

qu'est-ce que c'est?	what is it?
de quelle couleur?	what colour?
qui est-ce?	who is it?
tu veux?	would you like?
qu'est-ce que tu veux?	what would you like?
qu'est-ce que tu fais?	what are you doing?
tu aimes?	do you like?
tu aimes lire/ chanter?	do you like reading/ singing?
qu'est-ce que tu aimes faire?	what do you like doing?
qu'est-ce que tu veux faire?	what do you want to do?
où est?	where is?
où sont?	where are?

Telling the time

quelle heure est-il?	what's the time?
il est deux heures	it's two o'clock
il est trois heures et demie	it's half past three
il est quatre heures et quart	it's a quarter past four
il est cinq heures moins le quart	it's a quarter to five
il est midi	it's midday
il est minuit	it's midnight

Activities and Games

French once a day...

Every day may be a bit ambitious, though ideal if you can manage it. Try and build some simple French into your routine:

★ Pin up the poster in a prominent place. Mark the days of the week with a paper clip. Note the weather each day.
★ Learn a few basic but useful phrases like 'pass me' or 'thank you' or 'let's go' or 'I'm coming' (see pages 2 and 3). Use them regularly, or at a set time, like breakfast, lunch on Saturday, or on the way to school.
★ Count things, like your footsteps, or kicking a ball, or while you lay the table.
★ Buy some simple French picture books or cassettes and have a cuddly bedtime story. Make it a special treat.
★ Play the recording in the car and sing along with the songs.

French corner

Create a French corner in your house or classroom.
★ Collect French things to put in the corner, like stamps, French books, French food, matches, menus and bills.
★ Draw and colour a poster of the French flag to decorate the corner. If you have a French pen friend (see page 10) you can keep their letters and photos in the corner. If it's a large corner, you could hold your French sessions there!

New French words

Before you start a game, spend a few minutes introducing the new words and phrases – but not too many at a time (they are on the recording).
Note: in French '**le**' and '**la**', mean 'the', while '**un**' and '**une**' mean 'a'.
For example:
<u>le</u> **chat** (<u>the</u> cat), <u>un</u> **chat** (<u>a</u> cat); or
<u>la</u> **tasse** (<u>the</u> cup), <u>une</u> **tasse** (<u>a</u> cup).

★ Listen and repeat the words. Clap to help pronunciation, especially the syllables of longer words.
★ Use the flash cards. Point to the number or picture and say its name clearly. Gesture for the children to repeat it.
★ Hold up cards randomly and ask questions, for example: **C'est le... bleu?** (Is it... blue?) so the children can answer **Oui** (Yes) or **Non** (No).
★ Turn the cards face down. The children can pick one out and say the word, or ask the question **Qu'est-ce que c'est?** (What is it?).

Label your house

Cut out the labels from the centre pages. Attach them with a re-usable adhesive like Blu-Tack so they can easily be moved around.

★ Stick up different ones each day or each week. If you leave them too long, they will lose their impact.
★ Make it into a game. Hold them out in a fan, face down like a pack of cards, and ask the children to pick one. They can say it out loud or repeat it after you, and then go and stick it in the right place.

★ Stick some around the house and ask the question: **Où est… la télé?** (Where is… the TV?). The children can show you.
★ To collect the labels, someone could say **Apporte-moi…le lit** (Bring me… the bed).
★ Make your own labels, too. See *French art and craft* (page 9) for ideas.

Apporte-moi…

Pairs game

For 2 or more players

This familiar game is especially useful to practise the words on the flash cards.

★ Shuffle the cards and lay them all out face down.
★ Take it in turns. Turn over two cards and say their French names out loud.
★ If they are a pair, say **Oui** (Yes) or **Oui, j'ai une paire** (Yes, I have a pair) and keep them. If not turn them back over in exactly the same position and say, **Non** (No) or **Non, je n'ai pas de paire** (No, I don't have a pair).
★ The player with the most pairs wins.

With very young children, use only three pairs to start with and work up to more. Older children could try guessing the card before they turn it over. Either use one word **Bleu?** (Blue?) or **Fromage?** (Cheese?) or a simple phrase like **C'est le bleu?** (Is it the blue?) or **C'est le fromage?** (Is it the cheese?).

Activities and Games

Lotto

For 2 players

Another fun way to practise flash card words.

★ Put one card from each flash card pair into a bag or box.
★ Deal out the remaining cards to the players.
★ Pick a card from the bag and say the word out loud in French.
★ The player who has its pair says **Oui** (Yes) or **Oui, j'ai… le cinq** (Yes, I have…the five). Give them the card. Other players say **Non** (No) or **Non, je n'ai pas de paire** (No, I don't have a pair).
★ The first player to pair up all their cards calls out **J'ai gagné!** (I've won!).

Packing a suitcase

This popular travel game is a lively way to practise the French words for clothes. (See the back of the board game.)

★ Take it in turns to say **Je fais mes bagages et je mets…** (I'm packing my suitcase and I put in…) and choose something to put in the suitcase, for example **un chapeau** (a hat).
★ Each person repeats the list and adds another thing, so: **Je fais mes bagages et je mets un chapeau… et une robe** (I'm packing my suitcase and I put in a hat… and a dress).
★ You might run out of memory before you run out of words!

Let's go shopping

This is a similar game to the packing one above, but you go shopping.

★ Take it in turns to say **Je vais au magasin et je vais acheter…** (I'm going to the shop and I'm going to buy…) then each player adds one thing, like **une tomate** (a tomato).

You can adapt this game to practise any themed vocabulary: seeing farm animals, for example: **Je suis à la ferme et je vois…** (I'm at the farm and I see…).

dining room	kitchen	sitting room
door	stairs	hall
rug, carpet	mirror	radiator
lamp	table	chair
basin	shower	bath
fridge	oven	cooker
spoon	knife	fork
radio	video recorder	TV
pencil	ballpoint pen	pen
glasses	toys	bicycle

le salon	la cuisine	la salle à manger
le vestibule	l'escalier	la porte
le radiateur	le miroir	le tapis
la chaise	la table	la lampe
le bain	la douche	le lavabo
la cuisinière	le four	le frigo
la fourchette	le couteau	la cuillère
la télé	le magnétoscope	la radio
le stylo	le bic	le crayon
le vélo	les jouets	les lunettes

la glace	le pain	le chocolat	le fromage
la tomate	le lait	la pomme	l'eau
le gâteau	la banane	la confiture	le jambon
le coca	les spaghettis	le sandwich	la pizza
les frites	l'œuf	les bonbons	le jus d'orange

1 un	**2** deux	**3** trois	**4** quatre
5 cinq	**6** six	**7** sept	**8** huit
9 neuf	**10** dix	**11** onze	**12** douze
13 treize	**14** quatorze	**15** quinze	**16** seize
17 dix-sept	**18** dix-huit	**19** dix-neuf	**20** vingt

rouge	bleu/bleue	jaune	vert/verte
orange	noir/noire	blanc/blanche	violet/violette
rose	gris/grise	marron	**0** zéro
le chien	le chat	le lapin	le cheval
la souris	**le canard**	le mouton	la vache

Les vêtements
(clothes)

Fill in the spaces from the
list of French words below.

Au Trésor! to the treasure!

For 2- 4 people.

A board game to practise lots of different expressions.

Key to characters

Superchat (Supercat)
a heroic cat

Inspecteur Gros (Inspector Fat)
a brave police dog

Monstrerat (Monsterat)
Supercat's worst enemy

Megasouris (Megamouse)
Monsterat's partner in crime

1 2 3 4 5

start here

Count to 4. Move forward 4.

Stop for your favourite TV programme. Say: "I like watching TV".

27 26 25 24 23

La sœur de Superchat

Les étoiles

29

30

Le frère de l'inspecteur Gros

Stop for a snooze. Say to yourself: "Sleep well!"

32

33

35 36 37

Stopped by Inspector Fat's brother. Tell him how old you are. Go back 3.

Run forward 4 squares. Say: "I like playing football".

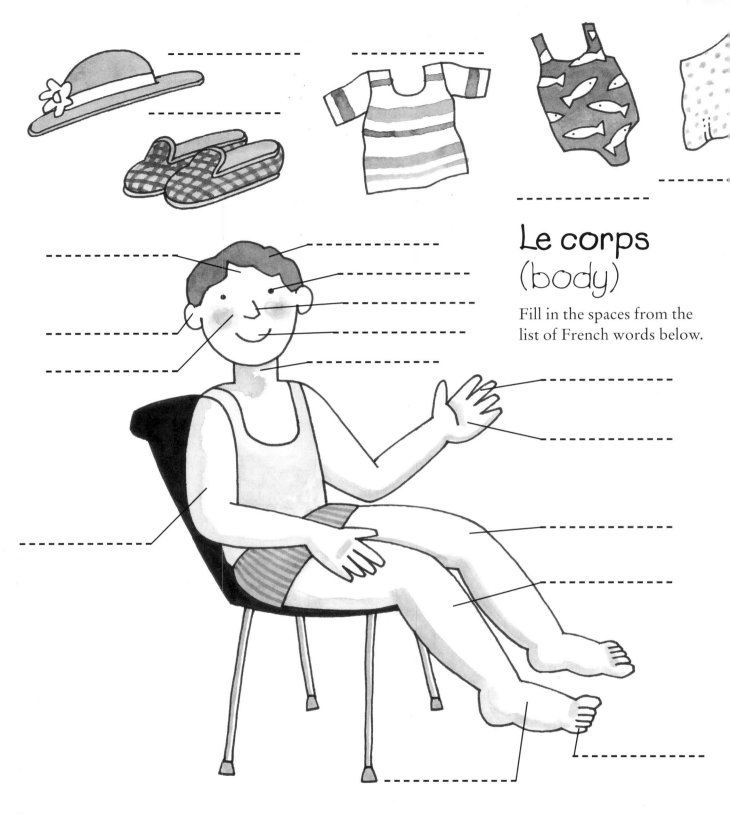

Le corps
(body)

Fill in the spaces from the list of French words below.

la bouche (mouth)
le bras (arm)
les cheveux (hair)
le cou (neck)

les doigts (fingers)
les doigts de pied (toes)
le genou (knee)
la jambe (leg)

la main (hand)
le nez (nose)
l'œil/les yeux (eye/eyes)
l'oreille (ear)

le pied (foot)
la tête (head)
le visage (face)

rouge	bleu/bleue	jaune	vert/verte
orange	noir/noire	blanc/blanche	violet/violett
rose	gris/grise	marron	0 zéro
le chien	le chat	le lapin	le cheval
la souris	le canard	le mouton	la vache

1 un	**2** deux	**3** trois	**4** quatre
5 cinq	**6** six	**7** sept	**8** huit
9 neuf	**10** dix	**11** onze	**12** douze
13 treize	**14** quatorze	**15** quinze	**16** seize
17 dix-sept	**18** dix-huit	**19** dix-neuf	**20** vingt

la glace	le pain	le chocolat	le fromage
la tomate	le lait	la pomme	l'eau
le gâteau	la banane	la confiture	le jambon
le coca	les spaghettis	le sandwich	la pizza
les frites	l'œuf	les bonbons	le jus d'orang

la chambre	la salle de bains	les toilettes
la fenêtre	le mur	le plafond
le lit	l'armoire	le fauteuil
le vase	la plante	l'aspirateur
le robinet	la brosse à dents	la serviette
le placard	le tiroir	la poubelle
l'assiette	le verre	la tasse
le téléphone	l'ordinateur	l'imprimante
la règle	la gomme	le livre
la clef	la pendule	le réveil

toilet	bathroom	bedroom
ceiling	wall	window
armchair	wardrobe	bed
vacuum cleaner	plant	vase
towel	toothbrush	tap
dustbin	drawer	cupboard
cup	glass	plate
printer	computer	telephone
book	rubber	ruler
alarm clock	clock	key

Finger puppets

Make the finger puppets on the inside front cover. They are wonderful for practising saying hello and short conversations.

★ Give each puppet a name and a different voice so they can 'talk' to each other.
★ Hide a puppet and ask **Où est… Georges?** (Where is…George?). Answer **Ici!** (Here!) or **Je suis ici!** (I'm here.)
★ Act the finger rhyme on page 11. Try and find other French rhymes.
★ Practise other language, like greetings, introducing family and friends, saying name and age, or please and thank you (see also pages 2 and 3). Keep the conversations short and simple. Add new language in stages.

Supercat Mask

Make the mask on the inside front cover.

★ Whoever wears the mask is 'Superchat' – who only speaks French!
★ Make sure it's a real treat to wear the mask. Children can wear the **Je parle français** (I speak French) badge too.
★ Build up the 'mask language' slowly. At first whoever wears it could just say

Salut (Hi). Then they could say their name **Je m'appelle…** (My name is…) or **Je m'appelle Superchat** (My name is Supercat) and their age, **J'ai huit ans** (I'm eight) and perhaps **Je parle français** (I speak French). They can progress to saying what their likes and dislikes are, what they enjoy doing, what day it is, and asking other people questions.
★ Whoever wears the mask could have a bonus, like starting first in the games.
★ Use the mask as a reward for winning a game.

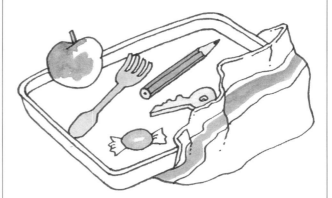

Guess what?

Use this game to practise new words.

★ Put some small objects on a tray: an apple, a key, a pencil, a fork, a sweet. (If necessary learn some new words.) Cover the tray with a cloth.
★ Uncover the tray and allow the children a short time to look at the objects.
★ Then quickly cover the tray again.
★ They have to try and remember the objects and say them out loud in French.
★ Try using the phrase **Il y a…** (There is…).
★ For a variation, put the objects in a bag and guess what it contains by feeling.

Activities and Games

Ugh!

Use this game to practise saying **J'aime** (I like) and **Je n'aime pas** (I don't like).

★ Collect small bottles or yogurt pots and fill them with various smells, like rose petals, banana, mint, coffee beans, soap.
★ Fill other pots with things to touch, like peeled grapes, a damp sponge, sand, a leaf.
★ Smell or touch something and say **J'aime ça** (I like that) or **Je n'aime pas ça** (I don't like that). Pull faces and make appropriate gestures!
★ Then let the children sniff or feel and tell you what they think. It is more exciting if they are lightly blindfolded.

Charades

Adapt this game to practise saying what you *like* doing e.g. **J'aime lire** (I like reading). Revise the phrases on page 3 before you start.

★ One person mimes what they like doing. The others have to guess. They can ask a question **Tu aimes lire?** (Do you like reading?) or give an answer **Tu aimes lire** (You like reading). The person miming answers either **Non** (No) if it's the wrong guess, or **Oui, j'aime lire** (Yes, I like reading) if the guess is right.
★ To practise saying what you are doing, one person mimes. The others ask **Qu'est-ce que tu fais?** (What are you doing?) and the actor gives the answer, e.g. **Je lis** (I'm reading).

Let's pretend

Use role play and little dramas to practise 'real life' situations, particularly shopping or introducing friends or family. Dress up and use simple home-made props to set the scenes.

★ Revise the phrases beforehand – this can be the show rehearsal.
★ For older children write prompt notes on cards, like 'You are a shopkeeper. Say hello. Ask, How are you?' or 'You are the customer. Ask for some cheese.'
★ It's fun to use French names and, as they do in France, **Monsieur**, **Madame**, and **Mademoiselle**, without a surname.
★ Keep it short and simple.
★ Below are two role play examples. Rather than simply reading them out, use them as a guide and let the children improvise.

These two conversations are recorded.

Shopping

Shopkeeper	**Bonjour.**
Customer	**Bonjour. Je voudrais…trois pommes et deux bananes, s'il vous plaît.**
Shopkeeper	**Voilà. C'est tout?**
Customer	**Oui, c'est combien?**
Shopkeeper	**Trente-cinq.**
Customer	**Merci.**
Shopkeeper	**Au revoir.**

Introducing family and friends

1st person (Michel)	**Salut Jean!**
2nd person (Jean)	**Salut Michel. Ça va?**
1st person (Michel)	**Oui, merci, ça va bien. Voici mon père.**
2nd person (Jean)	**Bonjour, Monsieur.**
3rd person (le père)	**Bonjour, Jean.**
1st person (Michel)	**Et voici ma sœur, Marie.**
2nd person (Jean)	**Salut, Marie!**
4th person (Marie)	**Salut, Jean.**

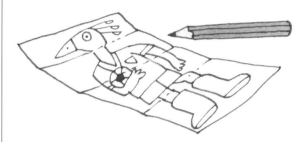

Heads, bodies and legs

Revise the parts of the body first (see the back of the board game).

★ Each player has a blank piece of paper.
★ Give instructions: **Dessinez la tête** (Draw the head), then **Dessinez le corps** (Draw the body), then **Dessinez les jambes** (Draw the legs) and finally **Dessinez les pieds** (Draw the feet).
★ After each stage, each player folds the paper over to hide their drawing (leaving a tiny bit showing) and passes it to their neighbour to add on the next stage.
★ The children could chant as they draw **Je dessine la tête** (I'm drawing the head), etc.
★ Once they're confident, the children can give the instructions. Older children could label each stage.

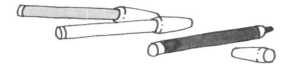

French arts and crafts

Apply art and design skills to learning French!

★ Make extra flash cards or room labels with the children. Cut pictures out of magazines, stick them on card and label them.
★ Make badges with special messages.
★ Make birthday cards, Christmas cards and cards for other special occasions. Here are some useful phrases:
  Bon anniversaire (Happy birthday)
  Joyeux Noël (Merry Christmas)
  Bonne année (Happy new year)
  Joyeuses Pâques (Happy Easter)
  Salut de la part de… (Hi from…)
★ Draw self-portraits and use them to learn the parts of the body and clothes. (See the back of the board game.) Younger children can answer the question **Qu'est-ce que c'est?** (What's that?) with the answers **C'est la tête** (It's the head) or **C'est une chaussure** (It's a shoe). Older children can label them too.

Bon anniversaire!

Activities and Games

Active French

Young children won't want to sit still for a long time. Here are some ideas to get them moving, but still speaking French.

★ Count while skipping or bouncing balls.
★ Play a version of musical chairs using the flash cards. Put one chair for each child in a row, and one card (e.g. colours) on each chair. While the music plays, the children walk round the chairs. When the music stops, call out one colour. The children may sit down on any chair except the one with that colour. The person without a chair is out. Take one chair away each time.
★ Use the songs on page 12 to dance and sing along to the tunes. Make up actions too.
★ Play **Quelle heure est-il Monsieur Loup?** (What's the time Mr Wolf?) to practise telling the time with older children. Stick to simple times at first. The wolf, **Monsieur Loup**, walks around the room and everyone follows, taking turns to call out **Quelle heure est-il, Monsieur Loup?** The wolf answers a time, for example: **Il est deux heures** (It's two o'clock) or **Il est dix heures** (It's ten o'clock). But if he answers **C'est l'heure du dîner!** (It's dinner time!) everyone has to try and escape when he chases them!
★ You can adapt this to practise weather: **Quel temps fait-il, Monsieur Loup?** (What's the weather like, Mr Wolf?). Escape if he says **Il pleut!** (It's raining).
★ You could also rename the wolf 'Superchat' and he can wear the mask.

Pen pals

A direct link with a friend in France, or another French-speaking country, gives language learning a purpose and shows that there are *real* people who *always* speak French!

★ You can write in English with some simple phrases in French. Exchange photos, postcards and small objects from your daily life. If your penfriend writes in French, note the useful phrases.
★ If you are a nursery, club or school, you can pair up with a similar organization and send group messages.
★ Exchange audio cassettes. You can hear your friends' voices and build up your stock of French songs and rhymes.
★ Using e-mail is more instant. If you have the right equipment, you can even send pictures and voice messages.
★ Here are a few phrases to start you off:
  Cher (*to a boy*) (Dear)
  Chère (*to a girl*) (Dear)
  Merci pour ta lettre (Thank you for your letter)
  Écris-moi vite! (Write soon!)
  Amicalement (Best wishes)

See also book *Pen Pals* from b small publishing.

Rhymes and Songs

Rhymes

Il pleut

Il pleut, il mouille,
C'est la fête à la grenouille.
Il pleut, il fait beau temps,
C'est la fête au cerf-volant.

il mouille = it's pouring
c'est la fête = it's the feast
à la grenouille = of the frog
au cerf-volant = of the kite

ACTIONS
- *wiggle fingers for rain*
- *hop for frogs*
- *wiggle fingers for rain*
- *open them out for good weather*
- *run around and twirl like a kite*

Un, deux, trois

Un, deux, trois,
Je m'en vais au bois,
Quatre, cinq, six,
Cueillir des cerises,
Sept, huit, neuf,
Dans un panier neuf,
Dix, onze, douze,
Elles sont toutes rouges.

je m'en vais au bois = I'm going to the wood
cueillir des cerises = to pick cherries
dans un panier neuf = in a new basket
elles sont = they are
toutes rouges = all red

ACTIONS
- *count on fingers*
- *march to the wood*
- *stretch up to pick the cherries*
- *pretend to pop them in your mouth at the end*

Monsieur Pouce

Monsieur Pouce est dans sa maison.
Monsieur Pouce est dans sa maison.
Toc! toc! toc!
Qui est là?
C'est moi!

Monsieur Pouce = Mr Thumb
est dans sa maison = is in his house
qui est là? = who's there?
c'est moi = it's me

ACTIONS
- *hide thumb in clenched fist*
- *knock on fist*
- *thumb pops out at the end to say hello,* **Salut**

Songs

Les animaux (animals)

Je voudrais un lapin blanc,
Lapin blanc, lapin blanc,
Je voudrais un lapin blanc
  Et un mouton.

Un, deux, trois,
Et voilà, un petit lapin blanc.
Un, deux, trois,
Et voilà, s'il te plaît, maman!

Repeat with **un chien noir** and **un cheval**

526002

Le temps (weather)

Quel temps fait-il aujourd'hui?
C'est très nuageux.
Lundi, mardi, mercredi,
C'est très nuageux.

Oh...il fait mauvais,
    Il pleut, il neige maintenant.
Oh...jeudi, vendredi,
    Il fait froid, ah non!

Quel temps fait-il aujourd'hui?
C'est très nuageux.
Lundi, mardi, mercredi,
Toujours nuageux.
Toujours nuageux.

Ma famille (family)

Mon père et ma mère
    Et mon grand-père et moi.
Voici maman, et voilà papa.

Ma sœur et mon frère
    Et ma grand-mère et moi.
Bonjour et salut ma famille.
Bonjour!

Les nombres (numbers)

Un et deux et trois,
Salut, et ça va.
Maintenant je dis bonsoir,
Bonsoir.

Quatre, cinq et six,
    Sept, huit, neuf et dix.
Salut et au revoir.

Manger (eating)

Les bonbons,
    Ah oui, j'ai faim.
La banane,
    Ça va très bien.
Le gâteau,
    Ça, c'est combien?

Le sandwich,
    Ça va très bien.
Au jambon,
    Ah oui, j'ai faim.
La pizza,
    Ça, c'est combien?

Les couleurs (colours)

J'aime les papillons,
    Mes amis,
Violets, verts et blancs.

J'aime les papillons,
    Mes amis,
Oranges et marron.

Bleus, rouges, jaunes et roses,
Petits papillons.

J'aime les papillons,
    Mes amis,
Violets, verts et blancs.

Les papillons = butterflies